Blocks of Time
Fulfill Your Destiny and Your Purpose

*How to block your time, achieve great success,
and...have fun in the process!*

Dr. Linda M. Campbell

Your Personal Guide to Getting Things Done!

DORRANCE
PUBLISHING CO
EST. 1920
PITTSBURGH, PENNSYLVANIA 15238

Dorrance Publishing Co
585 Alpha Drive
Suite 103
Pittsburgh, PA 15238

Visit our website at www.dorrancebookstore.com

ISBN: 978-1-6461-0872-5
eISBN: 978-1-6461-0063-7

Printed in the United States of America
Library of Congress cataloged

Blocks of Time
Fulfill Your Destiny and Your Purpose

How to block your time, achieve great success, and...have fun in the process!

Your Personal Guide to Getting Things Done!

Table of Contents

———

"Think for yourself and others will not

think for you.

Follow your dreams and leave a legacy

for others.

Block your time and succeed."

Linda M. Campbell

To Sons Eric and Brian

Preface

My Life, My Purpose, and My Destiny!

This book is inspired by a dream I had after giving birth to our youngest son, Brian. Although I wrote some details of the dream, it took me twenty-nine years to pen this story. Extraordinary concepts were revealed to me in the dream that inevitably changed my life. The concepts were inspiring and relevant to concerns I had regarding managing future activities with our eight year old son, Eric, and our newborn, Brian. Howbeit, the revealed concepts worked in my life in an explosive, positive way.

While in a mild state of sleep, recuperating from childbirth in a suburban Maryland hospital, my mind became flooded with thoughts of how to effectively manage my time and responsibilities with a second child. The daily logistics involved with raising two children, being a wife, an educator, and my involvement in church, school, and civic activities seemed overwhelming. The time commitment seemed enormous and challenging. Going forward, I would need insight and wisdom to navigate my life and my time. Little did I know that an inspirational dream would provide a blueprint for managing my life's activities using a process I call, *Blocks-of-Time*.

In the dream, answers to questions I previously pondered were revealed. The dream was methodical, peaceful, and exacting as the concepts of how to manage time and tasks unfolded. Insight on managing my activities using *Blocks-of-Time* as my time tool became paramount. It was a revelation! While the concepts revealed in the dream were not new, they were profound, lavished with clarity and understanding. The concepts or answers all made perfect sense. They were tenets I needed to understand and implement to better manage my life. The answer was to use measurable time blocks. Coupled with using time blocks was an increased honor and respect for my time. I was to honor and respect the time I had each day and not take time for granted. Therefore, in this book, I tell my story and how I learned to maximize my activities implementing the *Blocks-of-Time* process.

After my dream, many of my frustrations vanished. To institute a quality time plan, I had to adopt a new mindset. With that new mindset, I could plan and prioritize activities and schedule them into time blocks. Using *Blocks-of-Time*, I improved my use of time in managing personal and professional goals. In addition, blocking time helped me to improve my work-to-life balance. Using *Blocks-of-Time*, I accomplished more short-term and long-term life goals than I ever imagined.

Whether the time concepts in future chapters are new or familiar, it is worth your valuable time to read this book and implement the *Blocks-of-Time* strategy. Using the strategy, you can manage your life with less stress and accomplish more of your daily, weekly, monthly, and annual goals.

Introduction
The Revelation

Throughout my life, I have been fascinated with the concept of time. I realize we all have the same amount of time each day, twenty-four hours to be exact. I also realize that time is fleeting and it is my responsibility to use it wisely and prudently. How I manage my life choices, my tasks, and my activities is impacted by the amount of time I assign to complete each activity. So, I began to measure my time and activities in blocks, assigning a specific amount of time to complete each task. Then, I manage and discipline myself to plan daily activities assigning smaller time blocks within each twenty-four hour time block.

Fulfilling dreams awaits each of us. The possibilities are enormous when you block your time into specific time intervals and give your undivided attention to each task. The dreams you thought were impossible become realizable.

Let's examine some dreams and possibilities that can be realized when you implement *Blocks-of-Time*.

Imagine focusing your time using time blocks and fulfilling your dreams. Your dreams could manifest in one of the following ways:

You can begin a fishing bait business or write magazine editorials. You can open a family restaurant or open a bakery selling cakes and pastries. Other creative ventures are possible. Begin a farmer's market. Become an author of romance novels. Begin an online e-boutique from your home selling jewelry, books, clothing or other creative items. Photograph pictures and use your computer to advertise and sell them. Flip houses and earn a part-time profit. Learn a new language. Join an arts club, take a French cooking class and travel internationally. Buy that new vehicle you have always wanted and enjoy touring the countryside. Take time to visit parts of the world you have never seen. Become a professional dancer. Audition for television shows that showcase undiscovered singing or dance talents. Activate your vision and develop your business. Other dreams may be to become an aviator, sail a schooner, learn to play golf , return to school and complete that degree you always wanted, purchase a summer home or start a podcast. Write your autobiography or get a ghostwriter to write it for you. The possibilities are endless using *Blocks-of-Time*, planning, and effort.

Sometimes we make excuses why we can not accomplish our dreams. We think, I do not have time to dream big and do new things or that too much time has passed to fulfill dreams. Good news! While you have time and strength to achieve your dreams, you can block your time and pursue the dreams you still want to accomplish. If some dreams have changed due to circumstances or time, modify your vision or pursue other unrealized dreams. It is never too late to stop dreaming and working toward goals. What matters most is what you decide to do with your *Blocks-of-Time*, realizing your time is your life.

Prior to the dream, I managed time and goals relatively well, but inconsistently. Inconsistency caused me much frustration. I prioritized too many tasks and projects in a given time slot, which created conflicts with scheduling and completion of other planned tasks. For instance, when I scheduled a staff meeting, I allotted a specific time block to complete the meeting agenda. If I needed extra time, I allowed the meeting to extend beyond the scheduled time block or I scheduled a second meeting. In retrospect, these modifications affected my time to accomplish other scheduled tasks and affected the time and plans of the faculty and staff.

Unscheduled time blocks became an imposition on my scheduled time blocks and the time of others. Later, in business matters, I learned to set longer time blocks for meetings to have enough time to cover agenda items or I placed fewer items on the agenda. Today, I am consciously aware that time and life are synonymous and that time is limited and valuable.

Being somewhat of a perfectionist, I spent excessive time completing tasks. The result was frustration and procrastination, creating anxiety for myself and others. Later, I learned to maintain a standard of excellence, discarding the perfectionist standard. Perfectionist standards are unattainable and can cause undue stress and missed opportunities, as we attempt to do things perfectly or not at all. Excellence replaced perfectionism as my 'gold' standard for measuring quality. Excellence is attainable.

This book reveals the importance of time and its effect upon my life and perhaps, the effect upon your life. I call this new understanding a revelation. Formerly, I took time for granted thinking, "There is always tomorrow." I did not reflect on my past with proper understanding that the time that passed in my life was irretrievable. My opportunities for living life, love, marriage, family, career, travel, and formulating relationships were limited. Therefore, it was up to me to honor and respect the time I have been divinely given. I decided to live intentionally taking advantage of the time I have each day. The epiphany I experienced in my dream using *Blocks-of-Time* was astounding. Subsequently, incorporating the *Blocks-of-Time* concept into my lifestyle makes me live life purposefully. Valuing time makes me appreciate life even more.

This book is a testament to using the *Blocks-of-Time* process to reach your goals. Think of a dream or goal you want to achieve. Time blocks will help you organize your tasks and time to accomplish your goals. So, let's get started with achieving your vision and dreams for the future using *Blocks-of-Time*.

Chapter One
Purpose, Vision, and Goals

*B*locks-of-Time reveals a systematic approach for assigning time blocks to accomplish a plethora of tasks and goals, within a twenty-four hour day. The key to the success of the process is that you get to assign the time blocks. I will always remember when I discovered the *Blocks-of-Time* concept in a dream. It was a life-changing experience. The *Blocks-of-Time* process required me to prioritize my tasks assigning specific time blocks to them. During each time block, I devoted 100 percent attention to completing a specific task. The length of time of the task did not matter; the process was the same. Of course, this process took time and commitment to develop.

Blocks-of-Time required a 100 percent focus on a task. Now one task was not in competition or conflict with another. A task could last for minutes or hours. The time process allowed me to focus on the chosen task . Then, after completing a task or activity, I moved to the next activity. Since the *Blocks-of-Time* process was first revealed to me, it has empowered me to realize far more accomplishments than I ever thought possible.

Blocks-of-Time is not only about creating time blocks to accomplish a task. It's also about honoring your time and commitment to complete a task. In doing so, you actualize your vision and daily accomplish many short-term goals; thus, fulfilling portions of your long-term goals, your purpose, and destiny.

Fulfilling my daily goals helped me to accomplish many life goals, rather than allowing them to lie dormant as hopeful expectations. I learned to transform daily goals into measurable outcomes that required dedicated *Blocks-of-Time*. For example, if I had a goal to visit a city, I planned the event, then set a time frame to visit and return from the city within a specified block of time. I could incorporate more time into the time block to visit parks or museums, to shop, dine, attend plays or sports events.

By using *Blocks-of-Time*, I achieved whatever goals I planned and often achieved more than planned. Designating planned *Blocks-of-Time* to tasks enabled me to fulfill my goals. A definite benefit, I was not in conflict with my time blocks to complete other goals. Intentionally, I plan events and activities using measurable *Blocks-of-Time*.

Blocks-of-Time is also about living life successfully by developing an appreciation for your time. Like the waves of the sea, time is constantly moving at a pace you and I cannot control. By creating time blocks, you can achieve more of your daily life goals. When emergencies or unexpected events occur, you can execute flexibility by modifying or re-assigning your scheduled time blocks.

The Purpose of *Blocks-of-Time*

My purpose is to inform others how to intentionally create time blocks and become successful at using them. In future chapters, I address several pertinent components resident in the *Blocks-of-Time* process that can potentially turn your dreams into realities. These components involve a vision, goal setting, scheduling, planning, purpose, self-discipline, priorities, flexibility, leadership, decision making, choices, commitment, expectations, exchanges, resources, practice, and assessment. This list sounds comprehensive if viewed as separate components. However, the *Blocks-of-Time* process seamlessly integrates each component.

Purposeful Living

Let's take a closer look at life and purposeful living. Life lived without purpose is frustrating. Each of us strives to know what to do with our time and our lives on any given day. Most of us work and have responsibilities that require a certain amount of time. But, are you allotting other time blocks to realize personal dreams and goals? I eventually realized that work and responsibilities do not destroy my goals or dreams nor do they require all of my time. I control my time blocks and my activities through my thoughts and actions. I make decisions that help me realize my goals and dreams, or I can make decisions that potentially destroy them. Life is constantly changing, opportunities arise daily. Therefore, I am the change agent to make decisions and manage what happens in my life. Other people are not to blame for my dreams that die. I am responsible for that.

I have learned to relax and move forward in a purposeful direction with a plan and patience. I listen to my heart (inner self) and pursue my desires, hopes and dreams. I imagine the vision and my end goal manifested. Having a mental picture of the vision works. Some people create literal vision boards so they can keep an image before them. It works. For me, I imagine, write, and speak the vision; then, I set goals and make decisions that take me in the direction of my vision.

We can realize our visions, in the midst of our responsibilities, if we plan properly, set goals, and exercise patience. I am not an advocate of neglecting responsibilities or family. Rather, when I have a vision, I find ways to accomplish the vision and take care of my responsibilities instituting effective planning, gathering needed resources, and setting aside time blocks. Blaming or hurting others for not realizing or pursuing our past dreams is often an excuse for non-purposeful living. Purposeful living begins each day and goes forward with a goal, a plan, effort and time. You are the only one who can take charge of your life goals.

Often when I think reflectively, a vision, ideas and creativity emerge. At the outset, the vision may seem impossible. However, it may be for the future. The vision and ideas require me to link short-term goals and plans to a long-term vision. From experience and research, I learned successful companies follow a similar strategy when they cast a company vision, a mission statement, and set measurable goals working as an executive team. The company's vision may require years to accomplish. After the direction is set to fulfill the company's vision, the employees work diligently and intentionally accomplishing measurable company goals in *Blocks-of-Time*.

In the Bible in Habbukkak 2:2, it is written, "Then the Lord answered me and said: Write the vision, and make it plain upon tables, that he may run that readeth it". Writing your vision and setting time blocks are important.

The Vision

After my dream about blocking time, I wrote the vision (the revelation). I imagined how my life and family activities could flow if I assigned *Blocks-of-Time* to my daily schedule. Strategically, I needed a clear vision, something I could document, read, and re-read to keep the vision before me and to remind myself to block my daily activities into purpose-driven scheduled *Blocks-of-Time*. The result was, I wrote the vision—realized the dream and wrote this book.

When our children were young, my vision was to successfully navigate my life with two children, a spouse, a career and church, civic, and social activities. Using *Blocks-of-Time*, I was able to navigate many activities and responsibilities such as, career and family. As new opportunities occurred, I assessed each opportunity and decided if I could block the time required to complete the task and assemble the necessary resources. If I decided yes, then I pursued the task using the *Blocks-of-Time* process. When the children were in school, to successfully prepare for work and school, daily I used organizational skills, necessary resources, and blocked time to physically leave the house and get to my destination.

Once again, when our children were young, one being an infant, I had to have a daily plan to get to the babysitter, school, and work. If I forgot to pack diapers when I took our son to the babysitter, I needed an alternate plan to get them. I could interrupt my work schedule, leave work, buy diapers, and take them to the sitter—not a practical solution, or simply keep extra diapers in my automobile trunk and with the babysitter.

Organizationally, I knew using time blocks wisely would help me to make all the life pieces work together, and it did. I simply learned to block my time, pre-plan, and schedule activities into time blocks. With that, planning became easier. For example, ease in cooking required me to food shop in bulk and have needed supplies at home. Before using the *Blocks-of-Time* process, completing household responsibilities was a chore. I seemed to never finish. Also, writing manuscripts and course papers seemed to take forever, and often they were delayed. Later, when I began to set specific measurable time blocks for writing and other responsibilities, with expected end goals, I accomplished more in shorter periods of time.

Raising children also required a plan and dedicated time blocks. My days of making intermittent quick stops for purchases at grocery stores, at my discretion, changed when I had children. With children, we kept larger quantities of food and supplies at home. Our older son had to complete homework and have clothes ready and prepared for school. The baby had to be cared for and fed. Fortunately, my husband helped me with family responsibilities. Together, we formulated a plan to work as a team. For the most part, we accomplished our goals. There were exceptions and glitches when unexpected emergencies or sicknesses occurred. However, we made our lives work by sharing resources and using devoted *Blocks-of-Time* to accomplish tasks. The challenge of making everything work was enjoyable, not a burden, because we could always see the outcomes. As is often said in sports, "It takes teamwork to make the dream work".

Goals

Again, once I established my vision, setting short-term and long-term goals helped me to accomplish my goals and vision. Setting measurable goals became essential to my success. I set goals that were daily, weekly, monthly, quarterly, semi-annual, and annual. Some long-range goals covered a five-year period. For instance, when I completed a master's degree, my goal required several years to complete because I took classes part-time. When I taught in high school, teaching was a long-term nine month *Blocks-of-Time* commitment. To complete daily activitities, I assigned short *Blocks-of-Time*, within the long-term time block. Each activity determined the length of a block.

Typically, my short-term goals would include tasks that required minutes, hours, days, or even weeks. For example, preparing a delicious breakfast at home for the family required a short-term block of time. Still, it was important to give my undivided attention to the task. While I was preparing breakfast, I focused on that action, completed the breakfast, and then moved on to the next item. When I did not focus, I would soon find myself distracted, perhaps burning the eggs and toast, or forgetting to put water on for tea. Whether short or long-term goals, each task required a devoted block of time. When looking at my long-range objectives, I had to prioritize my time blocks to coincide with my objectives. Sometimes my long-term goals were either advanced or delayed depending upon current priorities and circumstances. For example, if I received a job promotion, previously established time blocks had to be modified. I had to consider my family, new work responsibilities, IT system support, and the time blocks needed to pursue the new goal.

In summary, when I pursue new ventures, I analyze my options and decide what I want to accomplish, when to pursue it, and what is involved in the pursuit. The Bible refers to this process as "counting the cost"considering what is required in time and resources to accomplish the goal. When I decide the timing is right, along with other factors, I proceed in faith to achieve my goal dedicating the necessary *Blocks-of-Time*. Like me, you may not see nor understand how each detail will work. I encourage you to use your faith and meet your objectives using *Blocks-of-Time*.

Mentally Block Time

Blocking time is a process that first begins mentally. It requires thinking, pre-planning, prioritizing, and scheduling. Afterwards, the mental process translates into a physical action. Using *Blocks-of-Time*, I discovered I could accomplish more with a lowered stress level, as I planned tasks and assigned blocks of time to each task. For example, when our sons were in grade school or going to the babysitter, I mentally decided on outfits for myself and the children the day before they were needed. The next day, we could spend less blocked time getting dressed. The time required for getting dressed was reduced because of pre-planning. Establishing time blocks saves time.

Blocks-of-Time—A Constantly Moving Commodity

While time is a precious, limited commodity, time is also a constant. After my dream, I had a greater realization that time constantly moves. Time has a pace, a flow that is continuous and methodical. Time does not stop for you whether you manage your activities well or choose to mismanage them. Five minutes ago is part of your history, history you can never retrieve.

To illustrate my point, please imagine getting up at 7:30 a.m. to dress for work. When you awaken, 7:30 a.m. is in the present. Ten minutes later while dressing, 7:40 a.m. is the present and the 7:30 a.m. wake up time is in the past. The future is defined by the time that has not yet occurred, which can be the next minute. The future will become the present and ultimately the past. It may sound complicated, but it is not because time is like a continuous flow of water. The water does not cease to flow and neither does your time. Your past, present, and future are all interconnected and distinguished moment by moment as you flow from present to past to future and repeat the process.

Reflecting upon life using *Blocks-of-Time*, I share some of my personal and career accomplishments to show you how successfully this process works over time, associating time with tasks. I am a wife, the mother of two adult children, and am involved in many church, civic, and social activities. I served in several professional leadership positions in education and corporate business. Educationally, I was fortunate to complete a bachelor's degree, two master's degrees, and a doctoral degree in Education from well-known American universities. In latter years, I began an educational consulting company and became an educational leadership consultant and university educational doctoral advisor. In addition, I am an advisory council member on a School of Education university board. I provide these examples to simply show the more you block your time, the more you can accomplish. You may want to re-examine your life and see what you have accomplished, knowingly or unknowingly, blocking your time.

On a personal note, I accomplished much in life setting large time blocks. We celebrated our sons graduating from high school and attending colleges of their choice. Until my mother passed, I was her caregiver during the last seven years of her life. Simultaneously, I was active in school, church, social, and civic activities traveling nationally and internationally. I spent time hosting and attending family events, family and friend reunions, trips, showers, graduations, travel, anniversary, and other celebrations, which were the norm in my life. This brief list represents only a sample of the many activities and events I was blessed to experience in large *Blocks-of-Time*.

Again, we learn to appreciate timing in all things and to prioritize what is most important to accomplish during different seasons of our lives. As seasons of life change, so do our opportunities and dreams. Therefore, we learn to seize our moments of time and pursue priority goals and opportunities. Daily, we are aware that time equates to life. It is an epiphany, an "aha" moment, and a revelation to comprehend this truth in your heart and your head. You will view time and life with a greater appreciation as you pursue new expectations and strive to accomplish them.

People often ask how I accomplish so much. It is because I use the *Blocks-of-Time* method and learned to respect time. I cannot stop or slow down the pace of time. I must decide how I want to manage my life, my tasks, and my dreams. Now that I have a greater respect and honor for time, I enjoy scheduling activities in time blocks.

Respect Time

Respecting our time is the first step to successfully manage time and life. We all use time blocks to some extent daily, either purposefully or accidentally. We find that our success with time is dependent upon our attitude and respect for the twenty-four hour time span we have each day. For example, new mothers pre-plan and measure the time it takes to cook a meal, to feed the baby, or to visit a doctor. A surgeon blocks time to perform surgery and later to prepare post-operation reports. The physician cannot divide his attention and perform other tasks while operating. He must block the time necessary to devote 100 percent attention to the operation. Therefore, it is important to strategically manage *Blocks-of-Time* to fulfill goals.

Honor Time

For years I included too many activities into a limited time block, especially during the mornings when I prepared for work. I scheduled *Blocks-of-Time*, but then added extra unplanned tasks to the same time block.

The consequence, I was late to my destination. Unplanned tasks that kept me from meeting my time objective included: washing dishes, locating misplaced children's toothbrushes or misplaced homework, finding clothing items and children's shoes, or misculculating prepartion time and resources for shool concerts or athletic activities. Sometimes, I set a sixty-minute time block when a ninety-minute time block was better suited to complete the task. Consequently, I made necessary adjustments to my time blocks, not because I had not prioritized the major items, but because I did not factor in enough time to complete the tasks.

Each morning when preparing for work, my daily challenge became a competition with myself to schedule time blocks and then juggle that time to include the extra unscheduled activities. I added within the same time block. Usually, time won the competition because I could not complete all extra tasks and be punctual to work or to the next event. Time is constant. Time does not stop to accommodate anyone's schedule. I share these examples to show how time blocks can severely and negatively impact personal schedules when discipline and good planning are not incorporated into our *Blocks-of-Time* schedules.

Regarding business, when insufficient time is assigned to time blocks, there are consequences. When conducting a business meeting that lacks sufficient time to complete a planned agenda, managers may adjust the time block by extending the meeting or by rescheduling the meeting. However, managers or coordinators need to be sensitive to the effect these actions have on the time blocks of others. On a personal level, time block priorities change over time. For example, as our children became older, *Blocks-of-Time* priorities shifted from infant and toddler care, to youth care, to teen care, and now to adult relationships with our children.

Exercises

1. It is important to set periodic goals. List three things you plan to accomplish today, three things this year, and three things within the next five years.

_____

_____

_____

_____

_____

2. List one of your dreams. How much dedicated time (and effort) do you need to block daily, monthly, or annually to bring it to reality? Write a brief description of your plan.

_____

_____

_____

_____

_____

3. Life and time are synonymous. Why should you honor and respect your time? Write your answer in two or three short sentences.

_____

_____

_____

_____

_____

Chapter Two
The *Blocks-of-Time* Process

Another key component to managing time blocks is to decide how much time to allocate to perform an activity. To ensure that I remain diligent to each assigned time block, I depend on my watch, a timer, or my cell phone to periodically check the time. For instance, while working on this book, I am aware of my time block—-what time I began writing and when I plan to finish. Doing so allows me to spend more time on other projects.

Commit to Your *Blocks-of-Time*

I became committed to the *Blocks-of-Time* process. The concept was simple and intriguing. During my dream, the concept was so clear; I felt I would never misunderstand it nor forget it. I now understood artists, inventors, and singer celebrities who say their ideas or songs were revealed to them in a dream or vision. I know from research and from stories in the Holy Bible that dreams and visions occur. Based upon the *Blocks-of-Time* process revealed in my dream, I made a commitment to focus and measure my time. I learned to concentrate on one item at a time, blocking a specific time interval to complete a task. It was and is a process that requires discipline, planning, and scheduling. When a time block requires me to make an adjustment, I can extend the first time block or re-move a scheduled task from my list of things to do that day. I must strike a balance with my time, since time is constantly moving. Therefore using discipline and flexibility, I manage my tasks and activities within a given block of time and move on to the next task.

At the end of a day, I reflect on the goals I accom-plished. Blocking time keeps me accountable. Some-times, I am amazed at the number of goals I have completed in a day. As I effectively manage time blocks, I fulfill more goals. Now, I am intentional in scheduling activities and the time required to complete them. Others who use time blocks strategically can succeed in getting more things accomplished.

Dedicate 100 Percent Attention to Task

I learned the key to successfully using *Blocks-of-Time*. It is to dedicate 100 percent of my time to each task, perform that task well, and then move on to the next task. The process is simple and straightforward. Each task deserves quality and focus. Ah! How would

I accomplish this? At any specific time, every task, whether washing dishes or traveling to a sports game or researching a topic was its own task. I soon learned how effective time blocking was, and enjoyed the challenge of using the *Blocks-of-Time* process. You can experience a similar challenge when you set a time block and complete the designated tasks.

A definite advantage of using *Blocks-of-Time* is the 100 percent effort and concentration focus required to complete each activity within a time block. After giving birth to our children and having the revelation about time in a dream, I understood completely what was meant by devoting 100 percent of my time to a task using the *Blocks-of-Time* process. As a parent, when feeding the baby, I focused on that task and completed it. Afterwards, I moved to the next task. When I cooked dinner, that was my focus. If I had a break while something was baking in the oven, I could choose to perform another activity for a specified block of time. Thus, the *Blocks-of-Time* process emerged as an effective way to complete activities using time. Using options became part of the fun of blocking my time. I was accountable for working within my time blocks.

I began to view all activities as things that could be planned within a time block. Professionally, when I was late for an activity or meeting, I could decide to go forward and attend the meeting and gain the information or not attend the meeting. I was accountable. My options were to miss the meeting, reschedule, attend the meeting late, or elect to do something else during that time block. The choices were mine.

Judging Your Time

Since I am now acutely conscious of time, whether during the day or night, I can usually guess the correct time. In the past, I played a time guessing game with my family. They would ask what time it was at any given time and I would guess the time almost to the minute. While I could approximate the time, day or night, completing planned tasks in time blocks was still a challenge. During the initial stages of learning the *Blocks-of-Time* process, I used flexibility, until I learned to manage the time blocks process. Finally, I became more proficient in setting time blocks.

As a process, *Blocks-of-Time* provides a blueprint and a structure for using time effectively. While none of us executes use of time blocks with perfection, we can strive to use *Blocks-of-Time* consistently. Life is not perfect, so I do not condemn myself when I make a mistake with time. I simply make modifications to the time blocks.

Minutes Are Important

Minutes are valuable when used in *Blocks-of-Time*. I learned how effective and efficient it is to use time between meetings or before an event to check emails, talk on the phone, visit social media, telephone a friend or business colleague, or create a dinner menu. Minutes are small increments of time. Minutes become hours. Think of what you can accomplish in three, five, or fifteen minutes. I may listen to smoothing music for ten minutes and relax with a cup of coffee or tea. I can take a walk or run on the treadmill for fifteen minutes. Inhaling and exhaling fresh air for two minutes is great for increasing the flow of oxygen—a two-minute time block activity worth adding to my schedule. Yes, minutes count.

Flexibility

When interruptions and unplanned activities occur, instead of becoming frustrated, I shift my goals and adjust my time blocks. The process is so easy. Again, I recognize flexibility as "my friend" when managing time blocks. Conversely, flexibility can be an adversary to meeting goals if self-discipline is not used in the *Blocks-of-Time* process. As a mother and teacher when our children were young, I washed baby bottles, cooked dinners, graded papers, and prepared lesson plans for classes. Later when I enrolled in graduate classes part-time, I re-prioritized my tasks. I used additional resources and time blocks to accomplish my goals. It became necessary to intentionally plan more time blocks. At the end of the part-time five-year time block, the master's degree was completed. During this time, I was still active in my children's education and their extracurricular activities. My time blocks were limited and full-time study was not an option.

Narrow Your Focus

Some successful leaders and managers select three primary goals to accomplish daily. I also learned to focus on completing three primary goals daily. The other items became secondary. I narrowed my focus to block time to accomplish the three primary goals first. Then, I assigned time blocks to complete secondary goals. I focused on one goal at a time and blocked enough time to finish each task.

Prioritize Activities

I discovered the *Blocks-of-Time* process provided a framework for all my tasks. When I pre-planned the activities of a coming day, I framed the day by prioritizing tasks and assigning time blocks to each activity. I remember as a young mother how hectic it was getting out of the house in the mornings. Sometimes I missed my objective and did not get all I planned accomplished, within the established time block. Because life is not always predictable, I learned it is important to de-stress and have an alternate plan "B" when your original plan "A" does not work. When needed, adjust your time blocks by adding or deleting time from the block. Life and interruptions are going to happen—so we plan for them. By the way, navigating the needs of children and interruptions are synonymous. For example, sometimes I could arrive late to work because of traffic, sick children, or not feeling well. Initially, I felt stressed; then, I would have a cup of tea, de-stress, and move to the next task. My theory was to remain positive: God willing, there is tomorrow to improve.

In retrospect, my morning activities required more time than I typically planned. I could have gotten up earlier and extended the *Blocks-of-Time* I needed to perform my morning activities, or I could have gone to bed earlier. Being punctual is intentional. As stated earlier, the *Blocks-of-Time* process allows for flexibility and mistakes. By using *Blocks-of-Time*, I developed self-discipline, exercised patience, prioritized tasks, improved scheduling techniques, and learned to precalculate the time blocks required to complete each task.

Schedule Activities

As time passed, I scheduled my activities to effectively block my time. After pre-planning activities, I followed through and executed each task or activity in the designated time block. Later, I learned to provide extra time within my blocks to account for interruptions and unplanned activities. If my son forgot his homework or I forgot papers for a class, I estimated how much time was needed to correct the situation. If sufficient time was not in the time block to make a correction, I made a decision to create a new time block. Based on the situation, I instituted the best plan for the solution.

For example, once in rushing to work, I forgot a paper I needed to submit for an evening graduate class and it was the due date. My options were to leave work and go home during lunchtime to retrieve the paper to have it for class and not receive a low grade for a late paper, or elect to explain the situation to the instructor and submit the paper late and receive a lower grade. I used flexibility, re-prioritized my tasks, and retrieved my paper from home to have it during the evening class.

In other situations, I used time blocks to account for unexpected occurrences. When our children were in elementary school, they might soil their clothes during recess or spill juice on their clothes during lunch. I learned to keep extra clothing and supplies for my children in the trunk of my automobile in case of emergencies. These learned best practices helped me to save time blocks.

Self-Discipline

Creating time blocks requires self-discipline. While learning to implement the *Blocks-of-Time* process, I realized how important it was to hold myself accountable for my use of time. I found it both imperative and essential to use self-discipline when blocking my time. It was important to be honest with myself. I was the one to assess my time usage. Past minutes and events soon became part of history as the present quickly turned into the past. Therefore, through discipline, I learned to produce intentional results using the *Blocks-of-Time* process.

Exercises

1. What vision would you like to accomplish within the next five years? Write your vision concisely and clearly in twenty words or less. You can begin with, My vision is to...

_____

_____

_____

_____

_____

2. Success with time is dependent upon our attitude and respect for each twenty-four hour time period. List a situation when your "Plan A" with time did not work and you had to implement a "Plan B".

_____

_____

_____

_____

_____

3. Your purpose helps you to set your goals. List three long-term goals you desire to accomplish in one year, five years, and 10 years, respectively.

_____

_____

_____

_____

_____

4. Are you intentional in setting *Blocks-of-Time* for each task or activity? List five activities you performed today and the approximate time you spent on each task. Now write the time you could have spent on each goal instead.

_____

_____

_____

_____

_____

5. You may have brief time blocks available while waiting for an event to occur, i.e., a meeting, a flight, a presentation, automobile servicing. List three tasks you can accomplish in five or fifteen minutes.

_____

_____

_____

_____

_____

6. Punctuality is possible when we better manage our *Blocks-of-Time*. List three activities you were late to this week. What could you have done differently?

_____

_____

_____

_____

_____

Chapter Three
Blocks-of-Time
Opportunities and Challenges

I mplementing the *Blocks-of-Time* process requires giving 100 percent attention to each task. Whether the task requires minutes, hours, or years, you can set time blocks for completion. I pursued a rigorous doctoral degree program in Education at an American university. I am delighted to say I successfully finished the challenging program, especially the arduous dissertation process. While completing the program, I was employed as a school administrator.

Prior to entering the doctoral program, my husband and I agreed we would have to plan our time commitments. We knew it would take a six-year time block to complete the degree part-time. We planned our long-term *Blocks-of-Time* to accommodate family responsibilities, careers, study, classes, research, and travel. We did not want to sacrifice our family's quality time, although we realized the quantity of time spent together would fluctuate. After completing the degree, my long-term focus and time blocks shifted to other priorities.

Pursuing a long-term goal, such as an advanced degree, required a vast time block. Daily, I set short-term goals and time blocks to accomplish family and career goals. I did not ignore my family or professional responsibilities. My husband and I traded off certain responsibilities with the children, especially on evenings when I had classes. During this season of time, I blocked my time differently to accomplish my goals.

Results of Not Blocking Time

To appreciate blocking time, I had to envision what life looks like when time is not blocked. I began to identify scenarios that might result from a lack of planning or from setting inadequate time blocks. When I did not block time, I experienced feelings of frustration, procrastination, stress, and feeling overwhelmed. Without proper planning, I might miss important details in my haste to complete a task, by not scheduling adequate time blocks to complete the task. Also, others time blocks could be negatively impacted if I set inadequate time blocks. Stress was intensified by poor planning resulting in disappointments, missed information, and anxiety. Soon I learned the issue was not time, but rather how I managed tasks and time blocks. If you are stressed over being late, I encourage you to re-examine your schedule of activities and make necessary adjustments to your time blocks.

Organization and Tenacity

Using *Blocks-of-Time* requires organization and tenacity. Tenacity is the "stick-to-it-ness" and perseverance applied to get tasks completed. Tenacity implies a relentlessness to complete a task. To accomplish my activities and tasks, I assign due dates and time frames to complete my work. I use "To Do" lists, which work wonderfully. It feels so satisfying when you check off a completed item on your "To Do" list. With respect to the *Blocks-of-Time* process, being organized means you plan your activities, schedule your time, and have the necessary resources to accomplish your desired outcomes. I am tenacious in my efforts to not procrastinate when performing tasks I prefer not to perform, but must to complete a goal.

Perseverance and Time Blocks

Perseverance implies a determined attitude and effort to complete a task. Simply put, we often do not like to persevere, but must to accomplish anything! When our children were young, they had birthday parties. I might be tired from a day at work, but I knew the birthday party was a high priority and it had to happen on that one special planned day. Because we could never retrieve our sons' earlier birthdays, the highest priority on those celebratory days became making the day special and filled with love. Our children are now adults and the time for celebrating those fun-filled early childhood birthdays has passed. Now, there are new exciting opportunities to enjoy time with them and their families during the adult stages of their lives. The point is we established *Blocks-of-Time* to plan and organize activities, prioritizing what was important at the time.

Obstacles to Blocking Time

There are several obstacles to using *Blocks-of-Time*. Some of these obstacles you may recognize and others may be new to you. Unfortunately, obstacles can result in missed opportunities and failures. Several obstacles related to misusing or setting inadequate time blocks are: procrastination, disorganization, being non-committal, indecisiveness, feeling overwhelmed, insecurity, fear, laziness, self-centeredness, vagueness, negative influences, lack of faith, lack of punctuality, lack of energy, and a lack of discipline.

In life, it is normal to occasionally experience ill feelings or actions. The good news is all negative factors can be overcome. First, recognize them as obstacles to your progress. Second, quickly begin to realize how obstacles readily accepted as the norm affect our time and ability to accomplish goals. When I assign and manage measurable time blocks, I eliminate many of the obstacles, such as procrastination. Then, I forge ahead, despite obstacles or difficulties. You may ask how did blocking my time affect fear, or lack of energy, and feelings of being overwhelmed? The answer; when I view time and life as one, the obstacles that seem daunting diminish. I realize what is important in life is what I do with my time.

Multitasking Versus *Blocks-of-Time*

Blocks-of-Time creates a new way to look at multitasking. Multi-tasking refers to simultaneously performing several tasks at the same time. I used to try to achieve the greatest use of my time performing two or three tasks simultaneously, like performing a juggling act. Multi-tasking works, but not as effectively as blocking 100% of your time to complete a task.

Quality is often sacrificed with multi-tasking. When addressing the needs of children, it is difficult not to multi-task and divide your attention. Although, with multi-tasking, you do not devote 100 percent attention to a task. When multitasking, quality is sacrificed. Performing too many tasks simultaneously creates irritability, resulting in increased stress. Having a single focus using a specific block of time to complete a task well is preferred over multitasking.

Use Resources, Delegation, and Partnerships

It is important to use human resources and technological resources at your disposal when using the *Blocks-of-Time* process. In the past, I did not seek available resources, until I realized I could not operate successfully without requesting assistance. For example, if I had a late school meeting, I might ask a babysitter to keep our children. When a parent meeting was scheduled and my child became ill, I might ask another school official to conduct the meeting. This availability of resources made me humble and appreciative.

In business, I learned to partner with those who could help me accomplish my goals. Partners are a vital resource when new visions emerge or the amount of work escalates and we need assistance. On a personal level, formulating partnerships can also help you complete your goals.

Reading Success Using *Blocks-of-Time*

Setting reading time blocks is important. I am a proponent of reading and view reading literacy as a hallmark of learning. In a previous book, *The Miracle Study Guide*, I wrote a reading strategy for students who want to increase their reading comprehension. I recommended students 'pleasure read' a textbook chapter or material a minimum of twenty minutes per day prior to the material becoming required reading.

By reading the chapter or section initially for pleasure, the students read the material at their leisure. Later, when the chapter or section is required reading, the section can be re-read for comprehension. This process requires minimal time blocks for reading and comprehension. More importantly, it works. The more times a student becomes familiar with reading a passage, typically the more he or she learns. Repetition and practice produce excellence and proficiency.

Another reading strategy that works for reading a large book is to divide the book into chapters or pages and read a specific number of pages or chapters each day. Using time blocks, a two-hundred page book can be read in eight days if a student reads twenty-five pages each day (eight days x twenty-five pages daily = two hundred pages). A three-hundred page book can be read in fifteen days reading twenty pages each day. The process removes the feeling of being overwhelmed by the size of a book.

Using a systematic, consistent approach to reading is key to this method. After reading, you can use your time blocks to do other things. Using time blocks, the reading is accomplished in short bursts of time and the student still has time for other projects. If you meet your goal, bravo for you! If you exceed the goal and read more than planned, that is even better. Using *Blocks-of-Time*, the stress to complete the book diminishes. *Blocks-of-Time* and patience are keys to achieving reading success.

Examine How You Use Time

Occasionally, everyone misses the mark with time. Making mistakes in life is inevitable. I forgive myself when I err using time blocks. It is important to continue moving forward with new objectives and activities. My solution is to challenge myself to make better decisions in the future, using *Blocks-of-Time*.

Every minute is to be appreciated. Some people tend not to forgive themselves or others when they make a mistake. That is unfortunate because unforgiveness can be likened to a virus that spreads over time. It becomes a waste of our time, emotions, and positive energy in a world where time is perpetually moving. None of us have time to waste our lives stuck in unforgiveness, anger, or bitterness—feelings that waste our time and energy and impede our progress. I choose to move forward in forgiveness knowing circumstances in life change, people move on, events end, and children mature.

Assess Results

Assessment is important to any venture. Once the venture is completed, we assess the results to determine what, if anything, we need to improve. As an educator, I used to tell students to always review their graded papers to see what they needed to improve or correct in order to avoid repeating the same errors on future papers. It is important to assess our mistakes and learn from them. To accomplish a goal, I identify a task then block time to complete the task. Later, I assess my results relative to *Blocks-of-Time* to determine if I blocked enough time to complete the goal. The take-away here is to evaluate results, actions, and the *Blocks-of-Time* used to complete tasks.

Dr. Linda M. Campbell

Exercises

1. Think of a situation when you blocked time to accomplish a goal. Was your block-of-time sufficient to finish the task? If not, how much time should you have allotted?

_____

_____

_____

_____

_____

2. List three instances where lateness occurred and what you could have done differently with time.

_____

_____

_____

_____

_____

3. List three activities in the past month where technology helped you save time blocks.

_____

_____

_____

_____

_____

Chapter Four
Blocks-of-Time and
Your Personal Development

Value Your Time and Choices

How wonderful to live life setting personal and professional goals and using *Blocks-of-Time*. I enjoy spending time with family and friends. To preserve a healthy life/work balance, I block family time and activities as priorities. I live relative to the precious time I have been divinely granted, respecting and honoring time, realizing time and life quickly pass like a vapor. A familiar adage of mine is, "Do not waste your time." I encourage you to be intentional with each day's activities. If you want to have a special lunch for yourself, take a vacation, or take time to read to your child, then set aside time blocks to do those things.

Recently during a planned day of writing, I decided to take a break from writing and take a ride to do some light shopping at a favorite store. Afterwards, I had lunch at a local Mexican restaurant. I had a great time in the middle of a quiet summer day. I exchanged my planned work *Blocks-of-Time* for relaxation time, with no regrets. Later, I returned to writing and other activities. Consequently, what is done with life and time is always based upon our choices.

Establish a Daily Agenda

It is important to establish your daily agenda considering your responsibilities and goals. Each day I plan an agenda of activities to accomplish. Although, sometimes others affect my agenda through unscheduled meetings or unplanned activities. For instance, as a principal, teachers might stop by the office unexpectedly or a parent and student might require an emergency meeting with me, interrupting my planned agenda. Therefore, to accomplish my goals, I learned to manage my agenda with flexibility, adjusting time blocks. There is a saying, "He who sets the agenda controls the meeting." The pivotal point here is, I am responsible for managing my agenda. In each situation, I remain aware of my goals and time blocks and compensate for any changes.

Until I started blocking time, I was not always conscious of how quickly time and life pass. I discovered setting an agenda was part of the time cycle for achievement. I learned to say yes to some opportunities and no to others. Life is a tradeoff of *Blocks-of-Time*; therefore, I take responsibility for what I do with time.

Planning and Execution Using Time Blocks

Experience teaches that planning and execution are essential to success. Therefore, when you decide what you want to accomplish, plan it, assign necessary time blocks, and execute your plan. As a principal, I allowed co-workers and parents to consume more of my time blocks than I initially planned, resulting in having to adjust other time blocks. This effect on my plans and time blocks sometimes occurred intentionally and sometimes unintentionally. However, I was the one accountable. The real issue, I planned too many extra activities that exceeded the planned block of time. I could reschedule tasks or delay them, but never recoup the time that elapsed. Later, I became more proficient at judging time needed to complete an activity. I began using a timer during meetings and when working on a computer.

Use Experts As Resources

Perhaps you need to let go of a responsibility in which you are not proficient and find a trusted, experienced individual who has expertise in that area. For example, I asked those who understand technology interfaces to assist me in business practices. What may take me an hour to research can be resolved in minutes by an expert. Using their expertise saves me time to do the things I do well. Utilizing other resources also saves my time. I receive advice from others if it helps me to become more productive and effective. I am a proponent of learning from others with expertise in areas that may not be my strength. The use of resources protects your time blocks.

For twelve years, I filled the role of hospitality director at my church. After several years in the assignment, the number of participants increased to forty people, and I knew I needed help to manage the team. I enjoyed the position and the staff and did not want to relinquish the position. Yet, coupled with other responsibilities, I no longer could dedicate time blocks to properly perform the role. My lack of time for the director position began to manifest in less follow-up correspondence and fewer hospitality group meetings. Eventually, I realized I was not performing the job effectively. Therefore, when a kind lady approached me and volunteered to help me, I enthusiastically welcomed the opportunity to have administrative assistance. Her simple act of kindness removed much stress from my life and allowed me to remain in the position. I almost gave up the position and would have if I had not gotten help. Assessing my *Blocks-of-Time* helped me realize the value of managing transitions and assessing my need for resources.

Ways to Say No and Protect Time Blocks

Protect time blocks by saying "no" to some great opportunities. I learned to politely decline some great opportunities. I learned to respond honestly and politely with respectful comments such as, "I am sorry, but I do not have the time; or another time might be better. These responses are polite, acceptable and respectful to others.

When you respect your time, others will respect it too. According to our sons, who were employed in the hospitality industry, some hotels train employees to avoid using the word "no" when responding to clients' requests that cannot be honored. They prefer the employees use phrases and multiple word comments to respond to clients such as, "Not at this time," or "We do not have that available at this time; Can you check back at 3 pm?" Addressing adverse issues takes skill and sensitivity to avoid offending others. Using an old adage, "More flies are caught with honey than with vinegar". Choosing to be respectful to others and keeping a calm tone of voice requires less time to address an issue than if it is answered in an adverse or argumentative tone.

The Failing Forward Process and Time

In life, failing forward is a process successful people encounter as they achieve positive goals. Many books have been written on the Failing Forward process. Failing forward simply means, while attempting to fulfill your vision, failures or setbacks may occur. Rebounding from setbacks and remaining true to your goals, over time you will reach your desired goals. Use *Blocks-of-Time* to dedicate time blocks to reach your goals. Because you may initially fail at reaching a goal, it does not mean you should stop pursuing the goal. Success comes with committment to completing a goal and putting forth the effort and time for it to materialize.

The Wright brothers did not give up when attempting to fly a plane for the first time. They failed forward, making many mistakes, before they flew. Similarly, Thomas Edison experienced many failures before he developed a working light bulb. The repetitive process of trial and error combines the failing forward concept and the *Blocks-of-Time* required to succeed. In life, we spend our time trying to arrive at a certain result like an inventor experimenting with a new product or process.

There is much that can be learned from analyzing the failures and adversities of others who eventually succeeded in reaching their goals. They used *Blocks-of-Time* working relentlessly to succeed at their goals. Like others who have failed forward, I learned to dedicate time blocks to fulfill my goals, while working through mistakes to find solutions. Another example of failing forward can be witnessed in an NFL football team striving to win the Super Bowl. Living in a metropolitan area, we have an NFL football team that understands the concept of failing forward. They win games and lose games, failing forward as they adjust game strategies and tactics. If the owners determine the team needs a new quarterback, they make the adjustment. If a player gets hurt in a game, they substitute the player. They are determined to win and apply the *Blocks-of-Time* process and effort needed during practices. Then in the actual game, the players have four quarters (four time blocks) to play the game. Similarly, in the game of life, we use faith and time to persevere, failing forward, until we succeed.

Fail Forward Time Robbers

In life, the fail forward principle is invaluable for accomplishing goals. For example, initially I planned to write this book for adult audiences during a different time period, but later realized the reading audience was anyone who could benefit from the *Blocks-of-Time* process. What I considered as delays while writing this book became actual opportunities to expand the reading audience. Sometimes, I allowed my time blocks to be absorbed by other priority events and activities while I pondered my goals for this book. Therefore, the "time robbers" I thought were negatively affecting my time in completing this manuscript were part of the failing forward process. I knew time robbers such as procrastination and lack of discipline affect progress. Achievement comes through failed attempts, delays, and interruptions mixed with a relentless desire to accomplish a goal. The failing forward process is not desirable and is often accompanied by humiliation or some form of emotional or physical strain. You can choose to allow the uncomfortable fail forward experiences to catapult you to higher heights in achieving goals or you can allow them to immobilize you.

When a baby is born, the baby is inquisitive about the world and must learn how to maneuver his or her body. As an infant, our granddaughter was inquisitive about her surroundings, constantly exploring with her eyes and her hands. When she began to crawl, she found she had mobility. However, during the process of learning to walk, she would fall and get up many times. She was determined to succeed. What a wonderful example of joy, perseverance, and determination when you watch a child strive to reach a goal and succeed.

Evaluate Your Time and Priorities

Yesterday is history. Even five minutes ago is history. Time moves forward whether desired or not. I have learned to use the following cliché: The sun will rise and shine tomorrow whether it is visible or not. The point is that life is perpetual and time does not stop for any of us. What we choose to do with time affects our lives. Today's circumstances will become tomorrow's history. I learned not to take my life so seriously, but to block enough time to set and accomplish my goals using the *Blocks-of-Time* process. Adversity builds and prepares you for next steps in life. Knowing your priorities affects what you do with time. Years ago when our children were sick, my husband and I exchanged our work priorities to spend time at home with our children while they recuperated. Reallocating our *Blocks-of-Time* to accommodate the illness became our highest priority. Work and other obligations took a secondary role. Once the illness subsided, our priorities re-shifted.

Plan, Evaluate, and Execute

In summary, you can plan how to spend your time each day, then evaluate the plan and execute it. Improved planning and scheduling of time blocks and tasks gives you more control over your life and helps you maintain a positive mental attitude. This formula requires you to evaluate daily goals, plan, and execute the plan using *Blocks-of-Time*.

Exercises

1. During a twenty-four hour period, we experience time robbers. List three time robbers that keep you from reaching your goals.

_____

_____

_____

_____

_____

2. Flexibility is a key to blocking your time when you schedule multiple activities. List three activities and explain how you will accomplish them successfully.

_____

_____

_____

_____

_____

3. Considering your work and home time blocks, name an inspiring opportunity you declined because of the required time.

_____

_____

_____

_____

_____

4. Name a major event you planned and executed. What block of time did it take to accomplish this goal?

_____

_____

_____

_____

_____

5. How is time your asset?

_____

_____

_____

_____

6. What goal have you attempted repeatedly before achieving success? Did you fail forward in accomplishing the goal?

_____

_____

_____

_____

Chapter Five
Be the Leader Over Your Time and Activities

You can become a leader over your time and your activities. You can plan and strategize what you want to accomplish considering the time blocks you have available. It is interesting how we strive to manage "time", as if time can be controlled. How do we manage an infinite commodity that does not ask us for permission to begin or end? After experiencing my dream on *Blocks-of-Time*, I realized I am the leader over my activities and goals, relative to time. Leading implies having a vision to accomplish a goal. Then, through planning, scheduling, organizing, and setting measurable goals with time frames I accomplish my goal.

Time is a constant, an independent variable. Factors pivot around time blocks, but cannot change the flow of time. Thus, during any given time period, I control my events and activities relative to time and circumstances surrounding my life. I can expedite activities, exercise patience, or just adjust my schedule. Nevertheless, I cannot stop time. In the Bible,

Joshua asked God to stop time during a battle (Joshua 10:12) and God did. For the rest of us, the way we effectively use time is to manage activities and goals blocking our time.

I came to the realization I am the leader of my life pursuits and the manager of my *Blocks-of-Time*. When hindrances occur that affect time blocks, my options are to remove the hindrances, change them, minimize them, or modify the plan. My outcomes reflect the decisions I make. For example, when attending a class, a dedicated block of time for the class was scheduled. I could either attend the class during the scheduled time block or miss the class. Class time was not the time to clean the house or arrange a meeting. Scheduled *Blocks-of-Time* helped me to effectively manage my goals.

Non-productivity is a Time Waster

Opportunities can pass us by if we choose to be non-productive and waste time. Our minds and bodies need to be productive, accomplishing goals—productivity is an exhilarating feeling and fosters a sense of self-esteem and growth. When mentally and physically productive, your *Blocks-of-Time* are used to create, organize, prepare, work, invest, or to do anything else you desire. Non-productivity is a destroyer of goals. It robs you of your limited time blocks. Non-productivity causes a waste of precious time—your life. Being comfortable and not pushing yourself to do what you desire to do can result in defeat. Others are affected by our non-productivity, whether in our homes or at work. We have a limited number of hourly time blocks daily, and non-productivity is a time robber.

Let's review a scenario. If your scheduled day typically begins at 7:30 a.m. and you chose to sleep until 10:00 a.m., how many *Blocks-of-Time* have passed and what is the impact? For instance, a student could miss two or three classes of instruction and the associated knowledge. For the employee, arriving late to work may mean someone else might have to assume your responsibilities. Chronically late employees may lose their jobs. Our gifts and talents are too valuable to waste being non-productive. Strategies, effort, work, rest, and relaxation are all great, but must be balanced. All activities require separate *Blocks-of-Time*.

Winning in life is a choice. Winning requires a decision, faith, and action. Therefore, winners do not have time to be non-productive. Winners are motivated by accomplishment. They are leaders over their time blocks. Therefore, manage your *Blocks-of-Time* strategizing, setting goals, and getting things accomplished, with an excellence standard. Anything worth doing is worth doing well.

Exercises

1. What project are you attempting that is not working? What can you do using time blocks to reach your goal?

_____

_____

_____

_____

_____

2. We are leaders over our *Blocks-of-Time*. Briefly describe what being a leader over time means to you.

_____

_____

_____

_____

_____

Chapter Six

Blocks-of-Time Affects Sleep, the Body, and Stress

Before my dream about *Blocks-of-Time*, I sometimes viewed time as a burden because I did not manage time blocks properly. My inner peace was enhanced as I changed my attitude toward time and began separating my activities into *Blocks-of-Time*. Any time mishandled or lost was irretrievable. Although we can never control time, we can control activities and manage our time blocks.

Sleep

Often, those of us who are challenged with demanding careers, family commitments, and other life demands persevere to complete all scheduled activities. While this approach is a lofty goal, it is often accomplished with a lack of sleep and sometimes to the detriment of our health and inner peace. Having a family and a career, sleep used to be a simple pleasure I longed for after completing the many demands of the day. Sometimes after the day's activities completed, I would immediately be ready to fall asleep. I spent too few hours sleeping to accommodate a good work to life balance. Later, I learned to value my time to sleep and intentionally set aside more *Blocks-of-Time* for sleep.

We know the body requires a certain amount of sleep daily. Medical experts suggest getting six to eight hours of sleep each night. The amount can vary according to the individual. I think most of us would acknowledge sleep as essential to functioning properly during the day. When I need more sleep, I can purposely go to bed fifteen to thirty minutes earlier at night. To improve my sleep, I might turn off the television and put my cell phone away until morning to sleep more soundly. Each person can practice setting sleep parameters and actions that benefit them during their sleep *Blocks-of-Time*. In life, you must prioritize what works best for your time blocks during different seasons of life. Then, discipline yourself to honor your *Blocks-of-Time*.

The Body

To obtain a sense of peace, tranquility and bodily well-being after a busy day, I block time and do something for myself. This might include walking, exercising, shopping, watching television, reading, etc. You may have other positive things you do to relax. When adequate sleep, proper nutrition, and peace with family and friends are introduced into your life, you have a stronger resolve. Avoid doing things to the body that leave long-term damage.

Stress or Calmness

By intentionally creating calmness in our lives, we reduce stress. Using *Blocks-of-Time* is an effective means to good planning and reducing stress. What a wonderful experience to operate in a peaceful, calm manner. The challenge is how do you remain contented and still take care of your responsibilities and keep your peace? It is accomplished, in part, by dividing your time into organized *Blocks-of-Time*.

It is documented by medical professionals that stress can be harmful to our bodies. A chemical called cortisol is released into the body when we are under stress. According to some medical reports, this chemical can contribute to heart attacks, strokes, anxiety, depression, etc. When under stress, sometimes we perform tasks in a perfunctory manner, not conscious of our actions. We also waste time repeating activities when under stress. Have you ever moved an item at your home or in your work place only to realize later you forgot where you moved it? For example, I had a habit of taking off my eyeglasses and inadvertently leaving them in various locations at home or in the office. My forgetfulness resulted from rushing and attempting to perform too many projects in too little time, often creating stress. I did not adequately block time to focus on a single task. Focusing on the task at hand during a specific time block is important. Life can become more organized and enjoyable using *Blocks-of-Time*.

Stress Relief for Couples Using Time Blocks

For married couples, creating a time block for a date night can benefit a relationship. Spouses can create time blocks to build their marriage relationships. Couples can set aside dedicated time blocks to attend a movie, visit a pier, sit in the park, picnic, or dine out. It is important to block time to do something you both enjoy since relationships need quality time. When funds are flowing, dining, plays, concerts, and travel are options. The point is to use your *Blocks-of-Time* well. For parents needing more time together, intentionally block time as a couple. Parents can set a bedtime for their children that is mutually beneficial to the children's health and wellbeing and allows parents to dedicate some quality time for themselves.

Exercises

1. A respect for time and life is important because your time is fleeting every moment. What can you do with a block of time that is enjoyable to you?

_____

_____

_____

_____

_____

2. We are leaders over our time and activities. Give one example of how you can be the leader over your time and a future activity.

_____

_____

_____

_____

_____

3. How much sleep do you average each night? Would you like more sleep? If so, what can you do to change your habits and routines to get more quality sleep?

_____

_____

_____

_____

_____

4. Using resources, we can save time blocks. Identify one major item where you use resources to help you save time blocks.

_____

_____

_____

_____

_____

Chapter Seven
Personal Reflections On Time Blocks

These reflections are intended to help you become more successful in planning and executing your unrealized goals and dreams using *Blocks-of-Time*. The *Blocks-of-Time* process is exhilarating and can become second nature to anyone who diligently uses it. I literally enjoy focusing on single tasks in a Block-of-Time. I challenge myself to see if I can keep on task within a time block. The *Blocks-of-Time* process is both contagious and motivational.

We set time blocks to accommodate our busy lives. Life can be pressured, euphoric, and even chaotic. Pressured and unscheduled situations occur in life, just as emergencies occur. Life is busy and has consequences and rewards. Using a metaphorical quote, "Physician, heal thyself." I know what works in my life when I have a myriad of demands and activities on my schedule. I go into a super-efficient mode to accomplish my goals using time blocks to accomplish tasks.

I recommend using time blocks to build and maintain personal and professional relationships when under pressure. I was guilty of sometimes allowing my stress over situations to show in agitation and impatience. On a positive note, I learned to be more aware of my actions and minimized giving short answers to others. This was a process that took time as I learned to better manage time blocks to tasks. As a high school principal, I truly had to maintain control in my daily attitude. I began to schedule fewer activities during the day, delegate more activities and tasks when possible, and partner with others as resources or experts.

It is also important to set *Blocks-of-Time* to create personal time with your spouse, children, family, and for yourself. Each member of the family is important and deserves some of your time. Establishing personal time blocks are important priorities in life for family, friends, and for relaxation and reflection.

Work and relaxation are important in your life. Work is easily committed to as a necessity for your livlihood. Relaxation deserves time blocks also to create balance in your life. Each person decides what is a relaxation priority for him or her. It is important to pursue what you desire for your life and set aside time blocks to measure your success.

Time becomes history a moment after it occurs. The reality of that thought is both astonishing and sobering when it comes to setting time blocks and priorities. Understanding you cannot retrieve a minute that passes, you intentionally plan your time blocks. Therefore, be a leader over your time and activities.

Be aware of time robbers affecting your time. I think we can agree that technology and social media are necessary tools in today's environment. However, cell phone calls, texting, emails, and searching social media platforms can become time robbers. In addition, they can be distracting when in competition with family and work activities.

Blocks-of-Time Sample Day

Rachael is a 31 year old insurance claims agent who teleworks from home. She is a part-time college student and is married. Her husband is a lawyer with a private business from home. Rachael does her husband's accounting books at night. They have a 10 year-old son. Sometimes Rachael travels for her business or goes in to the office. Other times she teleworks from home. Her son's school is 15 minutes from home.

Agenda Schedule

7:00 - 8:00 am	Daily hygiene, Prepare breakfast
8:00 - 8:30 am	Child dresses and leaves for school

8:30 - 9:00 am	Casual time for kitchen clean-up and coffee
9:00 am - 12:00 pm	Telework computer work for 3 hours (long-term time block)
12:00 - 1:00 pm	Lunch
1:00 - 4:00 pm	Telework computer work for 3 hours (long-term time block)
4:00 - 6:00 pm	Prepare dinner and eat
6:00 - 7:30 pm	Exercise and walk
7:30 - 8:30 pm	Dinner
8:30 - 9:30 pm	Business accounting for husband's business
9:30 - 11:00 pm	Casual family time
11:00 pm - forward	Sleep

Interruptions that required Rachael to modify or cancel her *Blocks-of-Time*:

- The son left his lunch and Rachael had to take it to school. She modified her time blocks.
- The computer buffered and Rachael could not get an internet connection for two hours. Rachael shortened the next time block.
- Rachael forgot she had a meeting scheduled in the office at 10:00 am. She modified her time blocks, got dressed and went in. She substituted the casual clean up and morning computer telework time blocks to dress and travel to work.

- Rachael missed several necessary ingredients to prepare dinner and had to stop at the market. She also worked later in the afternoon than planned. The dinner delay affected Rachael's next time block, which she had to shorten. Rachael cancelled her exercise and walking time block.

Chapter Eight
Conclusion

L ife and time are one. I value the time I have as I move forward in life. I have accomplished much over the past months following my agenda and setting time blocks to accomplish my goals, giving 100 percent attention to each task. I experienced distractions, interruptions, and sometimes pure exhaustion. However, being aware of time blocks, I accomplished more tasks than expected. I am no longer overwhelmed by tasks. Adhering to self-imposed time blocks is a rewarding work-in-progress. The "elephant in the room" is gone. The elephant is not using time effectively, missing opportunities and goals and not respecting my time and that of others. I plan tasks assigning an adequate Block-of-Time to accomplish my goals.

I highly recommend you commit to block your time and enjoy the benefits of peace, organization, and reaching your goals and dreams. Two minutes ago is now history. Going forward, strive to seize your time and make more life choices work for you using *Blocks-of-Time*. See you in the next book.

"Guard your mind with all diligence, for out of it flows the issues [positive and negative creative forces] of life" (Proverbs 4:23 KJV).

About the Author

L inda M. Campbell, is a Senior Doctoral Advisor in the School of Education at a prominent American university. Dr. Campbell is the founder and president of a private consulting group specializing in educational leadership development. Dr. Campbell also has over 30 combined years of educational leadership experience in K-12 and Higher Education. She has extensive management and leadership experience in private industry. She earned her Ed.D degree from The George Washington University in Education Administration and Policy Studies; an MA degree in Education Policy, Planning, and Administration from the University of Maryland College Park; an MA from International Seminary in Religious Education; and a BS in Business Education from Virginia State University. Dr. Campbell is a published author, education researcher and conference speaker. Dr. Campbell and her husband reside in South Florida. They have two sons, a daughter-in-law, and one grandchild.

successtimeblocks@gmail.com